I0774258

QUESTIONS TO ASK
YOUR BOYFRIEND

1. WOULD YOU LET YOUR GIRLFRIEND GET A TATTOO WITHOUT TELLING YOU FIRST?

2. WOULD YOU LET YOUR GIRLFRIEND SPEND A WEEK ALONE WITH HER EX-BOYFRIEND?

3. WOULD YOU LET YOUR GIRLFRIEND BORROW YOUR CAR WITHOUT ASKING?

4. WOULD YOU LET YOUR GIRLFRIEND GO TO A PARTY WITHOUT YOU?

5. WOULD YOU LET YOUR GIRLFRIEND PICK OUT YOUR CLOTHES FOR A WEEK?

6. WOULD YOU LET YOUR GIRLFRIEND GO ON A ROAD TRIP WITH HER BEST FRIEND?

7. WOULD YOU LET YOUR GIRLFRIEND BORROW YOUR FAVORITE SHIRT WITHOUT ASKING?

8. WOULD YOU LET YOUR GIRLFRIEND WATCH YOUR FAVORITE TV SHOW WITHOUT YOU?

9. WOULD YOU LET YOUR GIRLFRIEND CHANGE YOUR SOCIAL MEDIA PROFILE PICTURE?

10. WOULD YOU LET YOUR GIRLFRIEND BORROW YOUR PHONE TO SCROLL THROUGH YOUR SOCIAL MEDIA?

11. WOULD YOU LET YOUR GIRLFRIEND QUIT HER JOB TO BE A STAY-AT-HOME PARENT?

12. WOULD YOU LET YOUR GIRLFRIEND ADD GUYS ON SOCIAL MEDIA WITHOUT TELLING YOU ?

13. WOULD YOU LET YOUR GIRLFRIEND GO OUT TO HAVE A COUPLE DRINKS WITH A MALE FRIEND ?

14. WOULD YOU LET YOUR GIRLFRIEND CONTROL YOUR FINANCES?

15. WOULD YOU LET YOUR GIRLFRIEND TALK TO OTHER GUYS/GIRLS ON SOCIAL MEDIA?

16. WOULD YOU LET YOUR GIRLFRIEND STAY OUT LATE WITHOUT TELLING YOU WHERE SHE'S GOING?

17. WOULD YOU LET YOUR GIRLFRIEND ADD ANOTHER GUY ON SOCIAL MEDIA WITHOUT TELLING YOU ?

18. WOULD YOU LET YOUR GIRLFRIEND FLIRT WITH OTHER PEOPLE, EVEN IN A JOKING MANNER?

19. WOULD YOU LET YOUR GIRLFRIEND POST BIKINI PICS ON SOCIAL MEDIA ?

20. WOULD YOU LET YOUR GIRLFRIEND CHOOSE YOUR PASSWORD FOR YOUR PHONE OR COMPUTER?

21. WOULD YOU LET YOUR GIRLFRIEND GO TO THE CLUB WITH A COUPLE FEMALE FRIENDS ?

22. WOULD YOU LET YOUR GIRLFRIEND POST PICTURES WITH OTHER GUYS ON SOCIAL MEDIA ?

23. WOULD YOU LET YOUR GIRLFRIEND HAVE A MALE TRAINER AT THE GYM ?

24. WOULD YOU LET YOUR GIRLFRIEND HUG ANOTHER GUY ?

25. WOULD YOU BE OK IF YOUR GIRLFRIEND DIDN'T WANT TO POST ANY PICTURES WITH YOU ON SOCIAL MEDIA?

QUESTIONS TO ASK YOUR GIRLFRIEND

1. WOULD YOU LET YOUR BOYFRIEND HANGOUT ALONE WITH A FEMALE FRIEND ?

2. WOULD YOU LET YOUR BOYFRIEND POST ON SOCIAL MEDIA WITH ANOTHER GIRL ?

3. WOULD YOU LET YOUR BOYFRIEND LIKE OTHER GIRLS PICS ON SOCIAL MEDIA ?

4. WOULD YOU LET YOUR BOYFRIEND GO SHOPPING WITH A FEMALE FRIEND ?

5. WOULD YOU LET YOUR BOYFRIEND COMPLIMENT ANOTHER GIRL ?

6. WOULD YOU LET YOUR BOYFRIEND GO TO A FEMALE MASSAGE THERAPIST?

7. WOULD YOU LET YOUR BOYFRIEND TALK WITH OTHER GIRLS ON SOCIAL MEDIA ?

8. WOULD YOU LET YOUR BOYFRIEND GET A TATTOO WITHOUT DISCUSSING IT WITH YOU FIRST?

9. WOULD YOU LET YOUR BOYFRIEND GO ON A MALES TRIP FOR THE WEEKEND?

10. WOULD YOU LET YOUR BOYFRIEND WATCH YOUR FAVORITE TV SHOW WITHOUT YOU ?

11. WOULD YOU LET YOUR BOYFRIEND ADD ANOTHER FEMALE ON SOCIAL MEDIA WITHOUT TELLING YOU ?

12. WOULD YOU LET YOUR BOYFRIEND DELETE MESSAGES ?

13. WOULD YOU BE OKAY IF YOUR BOYFRIEND WANTED TO KEEP YOUR RELATIONSHIP A SECRET ?

14. WOULD YOU ALLOW YOUR BOYFRIEND TO GO TO THE GYM ALONE ?

15. WOULD YOU LET YOUR BOYFRIEND COOK FOR ANOTHER GIRL ?

16. WOULD YOU LET YOUR BOYFRIEND GIVE A LARGER TIP AT A RESTAURANT IF ITS A GIRL SERVING YOU ?

17. WOULD YOU LET YOUR BOYFRIEND TEXT ANOTHER GIRL ?

18. WOULD YOU LET YOUR BOYFRIEND CONTROL WHAT YOU WEAR ?

19. WOULD YOU LET YOUR BOYFRIEND CONTROL WHAT YOU POST ON SOCIAL MEDIA ?

20. WOULD YOU LET YOUR
BOYFRIEND DECIDE WHO
YOU SHOULD DELETE OR
ADD ON SOCIAL MEDIA ?

21. Would you let your boyfriend get a tattoo of your name ?

22. Would you let your boyfriend go to a strippers club ?

23. Would you let your boyfriend buy a gift for another female ?

24. Would you let your boyfriend flirt with another girl ?

25. Would you let your boyfriend comment on a girls post ?

THE END